MACHINE LEARNING USING FINANCE

Disclaimer

Table of Contents

What is Financial Machine Learning?

Understanding Artificial Intelligence

In order to understand what Financial Machine Learning is, we first need a brief introduction into what Artificial Intelligence is. Artificial Intelligence is, actually, a common theme in our society. From the bad guy in the movie to the interactive enemies in a game (a side note on noticing A.I. usually is the *bad guy*), Artificial Intelligence permeates our society pretty thoroughly. However, most of this is "limited" A.I.

Limited A.I. refers to a machine or program that has exceedingly limited capabilities. In fact, most of what you think as A.I. is also fake A.I. Fake A.I. refers to programming that simulates the experience of A.I. without being A.I.

For instance, when you see an enemy follow you in a game, it's not actually thinking. Instead, it's running a mathematical algorithm of "possibilities". There's a high possibility that when you are close that it may melee attack. There's a low possibility that it will throw a grenade. Otherwise known as proximity estimation, most enemy A.I. in video games are simply determining an action based on distance to the player and continued accuracy of player damage. This is "fake" because it simulates a machine that has intelligence, but it really doesn't have any.

Real A.I. could be compared to the "shadow" enemy or doppelganger in some video games. In these scenarios, the game has recorded your most common actions in the past such as: most common attack command, preferred distance, delay in the attack, etc. Based on this information, this "shadow" enemy builds a fighting technique that most challenges what you are used to doing. In this way, the machine has acquired intelligence on your fighting technique. In both cases, the A.I. is limited but one has intelligence and the other simulates intelligence.

Understanding Machine Learning

Machine Learning is *sort of* like Real A.I. in that it learns based on information that it is given. However, unlike Real A.I., Machine

Learning uses something known as Backpropagation. Let's say that a "shadow" enemy is made, what happens after it is killed? Normally, a new, strong "shadow" enemy is made later on in the game depending on the length of this game. That new, strong "shadow" enemy is actually built using the same information as the first one. The only difference is that you've ultimately changed how you play and the base "stats" of the enemy are higher.

In Machine Learning, such a "shadow" enemy will attempt to see where it went wrong in the first one. This could be done by looking at the same information but in a different light. For instance, if you normally relied on a heavy attack before but switched to the fast attack rather than the projectile, it would use projectile attacks to force you to play like that. The only difference would be that now it also could look at where the standard enemies are defeated, how they are defeated, and which patterns of the attack led to more damage. If this sounds a lot like "studying your enemy", that's because it is.

Backpropagation is the linchpin to how Machine Learning works in more complex environments. It takes wrong answers it produced and finds a way to optimize for the correct answers. There are Machine Learning algorithms out there that do not utilize this technique, and these are referred to as Feedforward Neural Networks. This simply means that the data is only being fed through the system from input to output with no output becoming the new input.

In fact, if you haven't already guessed this, the Real A.I. is a Feedforward Machine Learning mechanism, but it is not a Neural Network. Therefore, while it could technically fit the category, it's not generally seen as a Machine Learning algorithm. A Neural Network is full of nodes that break the choosing factors into their most basic components. This allows the network to move fast and come to decisions in a far more accurate manner. Therefore, unless the Real A.I. is created in a parallel programmed manner, it is not Machine Learning in the eyes of the masses.

Machine Learning in Financial Situations

There are numerous instances where you might utilize Machine Learning in financial situations. For instance, you could use them to come up with a more accurate forecast based on monthly accrued financial data. You could also come up with significantly better ways to predict stocks. This could even be used to determine who is working the best out of all your workers and which workers seem to need a little more… scrutiny. This might sound Orwellian, but it's important to remember that this is still seen as mostly A.I.

However, the truth of the matter is that most of these situations are usually handled with Feedforward Neural Networks. This is because FFNN (Feedforward Neural Networks) are far easier to create and less mathematically defined. Such a benefit for this is that you might see the same information out of a BPNN (Backpropagating Neural Network) because the FFNN takes into account new numbers when it runs anew. It is actually much more beneficial in many cases to build a BPNN, but it takes more time and resources to do so. It is important here that I clarify that resources also includes data acquisition.

9

Let's look at the worker example to discuss why I clarify this. In an FFNN, you might want to know when the worker clocked their breaks, the clock-in and clock-out times, and maybe their quantity production level during those times. This would be a rather decently sized dataset to work with to determine high-productive and low-productive employees. However, what if you wanted to try to find the **reason** why they were low-productive employees?

In such a situation, you may want to know a little bit more on the employees; information that's usually odd to ask about. For instance, if the issue is with some of the stock personnel, you might want to know sleeping habits, BMI, and general strength. In a Neural Network, the more information you feed it, the more accurate the results *can* be. That doesn't mean that it will always be that way, some data can harm your chances. The employee might be struggling because the material is heavier than they are or they don't move fast as a result of obesity. Then as a company, you might employ free access to an in-shop gym or create initiatives to get everyone in shape so that no one is singled out, which can be a PR nightmare and just morally bankrupt.

Predictions are what ML Algorithms Do

While some may argue differently, the ultimate goal of an ML algorithm is to make predictions based on data. This means that you have a machine capable of taking data and possibly making more accurate predictions than a top economist. That means that there's also a lot that it cannot do and, ethically, some things they are forbidden to do.

For instance, you might want it to give you a 12-month forecast of potential earnings. A Machine Learning algorithm can be made for this. However, it can't tell you how to improve that number. You could create a Machine Learning algorithm that determined which tactics had better success rates, but you cannot create an algorithm that will tell you how best to sell a product. Additionally, you cannot create a Machine Learning algorithm to take over the world. I've looked it up and there are simply too many variables.

Financial Machine Learning Weaknesses

The primary issue that occurs with most of the Machine Learning algorithms is with the dataset the algorithm it is provided with. As I mentioned previously, the more useful data that you give your algorithm, the more useful it *can* become. However, a good example of when a good Machine Learning algorithm becomes "bad" is a Google example from years ago. Google is a search engine giant that makes money by providing the best search results and, thus, being able to sell ad-space that more accurately reflect those results.

One day, something odd was found in the results of a particular pair of searches. If a woman searched for a name associated with a Caucasian male, the results would often return job-related websites like LinkedIn and Monster Job. If a woman searched a name associated with African American decent, advertisements and search results of criminal background checks would accompany the original search. The problem was not how the machine language learned but the dataset the machine was given a.k.a. women who commonly sought criminal records for African American men. The Machine Learning Algorithm was making an accurate prediction, but as humans, we would consider this morally

wrong.

Developing a Trading Strategy for Stocks

There Are 4 Primary Methods of Trading

Machine Learning can actually be used to determine what method of trading you might want to take part in. Additionally, it may even help you to open up your portfolio to commit to different types of trading strategies. In this section, we're going to discuss what types of algorithms can be used alongside the different trading strategies.

Ideally, if you are going into this first hand, you might want to perform a K-cluster algorithm on the past 5 years of trading information. Specifically, you want to include all companies that have lasted for over 5 years and exclude anyone that hasn't. This is called Cluster Analysis and it will find possible associations between the companies you might not have seen. An individual skeptical of the technology will only see how the machine can show coincidences, but there is often a good reason why some stocks rise at the same time.

Let us talk about Black Box LLC (not the real company) and Lee Memorial Hospital stocks (not the real company). There's no news associating these two companies, however, what happens when LMH signs a multi-million-dollar contract with BB LLC? LMH will now be doing a lot of business with BB LLC but LMH would have had a reason to make the contract. This means that LMH plans to do well in the coming time and BB LLC will benefit from this. Once the contract becomes news, everyone will want to get a trade in before their stocks rise and this, ultimately, causes the rise. However, what happens if this happens more than once?

There's often a lot of data going around stocks and it is difficult to keep track of contract renewals. Renewals are important because they can be a predictor of rising and falling stock between those in the contract. While knowing ahead of time what will happen in the deal can be seen as insider trading, using a K-cluster algorithm to see there is a periodic correlation is not. This is why it is useful to start this before getting started as it can help associate possible relations between companies.

Same Day Trading

While I did make the terminology make more sense, it is usually referred to as Day Trading. In such a strategy, you buy stocks and sell stocks on the same day. Therefore, if you bought stocks at 9 AM on Day 1, you would then likely sell such stocks at Noon on Day 1. This makes potential, devastating losses hard to come by. However, at the same time, you are not likely to be seeing a huge payout any time soon. Due to the speed at which Day Trading takes place, it is difficult to incorporate all of the possible machine learning algorithms.

Positional Trading

Positional trading is what most people think of when they think of investing in stocks. This is usually called the "buy-and-hold" strategy as most people will wait at least a week or more after buying in order to sell their stock. This is because these people want the big payoff or control that occurs when you are a majority stockholder. This majority stockholder is actually quite popular in movies as a point of contention. However, we'll focus on the bigger payoffs like those who invested in Bitcoin for free and became millionaires a few years later.

One of the key features to Positional Trading is determining what the best categories are. For instance, a lot of people choose Technology, Law Firms, Appliances, and Healthcare right off the bat. However, those same individuals will not understand what parts of those industries are best to invest in. This is a massive problem when it comes to developing a machine learning algorithm to make a profit as it needs to understand what is a good choice and what is a bad choice.

Trend Trading

Trend trading can happen for a few reasons. For instance, one type of trend trading is when you are trying to be socially responsible. If you believe in feminism you might go with supporting only companies that have a feminist calls. Additionally, another type of trend trading is if you see a popular piece of technology that is about to come out. If you pay attention to keynote speeches or if you attend technology conferences, you might know about a certain technology you think it's going to be profitable. Therefore, you might invest in a company selling those Technologies to cash in on a particular trend.

Lastly, the other type of trend trading usually refers to when you are trying to predict the trend line for a particular company. In fact, when stock traders talk about trend trading, this is the type *they* are talking about. The trend itself is a little bit more difficult to define.

Scalping

Finally, we get to our final methodology of stock trading. Scalping is a technique that is reminiscent of the actual act of scalping. In the actual act of scalping, one takes their enemies head and slices off the skin of the skull from the scalp. In much a similar way, scalping, as it pertains to stock trading, refers to the act of buying assets at their bidding value and then finding buyers willing to buy even higher using bid-ask spreads. A bid-ask spread is simply a difference between what a stock is bidding at and the asking price for the same asset. Therefore, if you find a stock that is bidding at $40 but then you find a buyer asking for that stock at $50, you can then have a bid-ask spread of $10.

The Plan for Machine Learning

Understand How Stocks Work

"a lot of people choose Technology, Law Firms, Appliances, and Healthcare"

Ironically, those categories are usually the most stable when it comes to investing. A good handful of people say that Real Estate should be included into this, but the property has to meet specific standards in order to grow. If you buy stocks into rich communities, unless that community is expanding, that community is likely to depreciate over time. The reason why those categories are the best is usually due to two factors; P/E and P/BV ratio.

In places of technology, you have a wide range of P/E. Let's get something out of the way real quick because shares and stocks can be quite confusing on their own.

A Share is how much the company wants to divide itself, which is announced by the company itself. Therefore, when a company goes "public" what they are doing is opening the Share pool to the public. At this time, they will release a specific number of shares. Essentially, they are selling components of a company to the public as a stock in the company. This stock is called a Share, as in you are getting a share of the company. A stock, on the other hand, is a collection of those shares. It's rather hard to keep track of 1 billion shares but if each Stock is made up of 5 shares, that's only 200mil stocks to keep track of. However! This is a story of all shares are stocks but not all stocks are shares. For instance, some stocks could be allocated to certificates and other parts that are share-like but are not directly shares. So, let's begin this by understanding how to calculate for shares since they hold the **real** value for stocks.

Let's first discuss BV or Book Value and to get this we need to break a company down into its most basic components and go from there. Let's go ahead and define asset and liability. An asset is anything that holds monetary value, whether it makes you money or you can sell it for money. A liability is anything that holds a deficit of monetary value, whether it costs you money to keep it or if it is a debt.

Let's say we are a software company and we're about to open up to the stock market. We know that we make $100 for every software we make, so let's use that as our basis. That $100, should we only sell 1 product, is called the **Total Revenue**. However, we only got that software because we had it made. If we have a software team and website, along with other items, that we pay for then this would be referred to as the **Cost of Revenue**. Let's say that for every product we sell, we have a Cost of Revenue of $70.

$$NetIncome = TotalRevenue - CostofRevenue$$

This number is called Net Income *and* is called **Earnings** when divided into shares. If there are 10,000 shares and you own 1 share, you make 1/10,000 of the Earnings as a result. This is the reason why finding out what a company is worth before you buy a stock is important. This is why you need to know the **Income Statement**, **Balance Sheet**, and **Cash Flow Statement**. You already know about the Income Statement as this is where you find the Net Income and Earnings. The Balance Sheet is where you'll find the Equity and Book

Value or BV of a company. This will be where your **Margin of Safety** is.

$$Equity = Total\,Assets - Liabilities$$

That equation is what calculates the Equity of a company, but the **Book Value** is a little bit different. Additionally, if you take the Market Price, the price that the market is selling all combined shares for, and subtract the Equity from it, you then have the risk. Therefore, if the Market Price for this software company's shares are a total of $1,000,000 and the equity is $20,000, then you have a risk of $980,000. This would be referred to as an extremely low Margin of Safety. While this bigger number is known as the Equity, when it is divided into shares it is renamed Book Value.

P/E refers to how much the company's market price is versus how much it earns, thus aptly named Price to Earnings Ratio. There are a few steps needed to get this number. I'm going to not only explain how to come to those numbers, but why you need to know them even though most stock "news" websites provide this freely.

To get to the P/E ratio, you must first find the EPS and that simply means how much each share will earn you should you buy it, named Earnings Per Share. EPS is calculated by taking the Earnings and dividing it by the Outstanding Shares number, which is really just how many shares are in circulation. To find Earnings, stock traders will take the Total Revenue of a company and subtract the Liabilities of the company. Therefore, the true calculation for this is:

$$EPS = (TotalRevenue - Liabilities)/OutstandingShares$$

The P in the P/E ratio is the current price for each share as it stands currently. The EPS is how much each share should cost as its' base value. Therefore, if a company says it's going to sell 2,000 shares at a total value of $10,000 then the value of each share is $5. This is the P side of the equation.

If we take the $100 for our software company earlier and turn it up to $10,000 and we do the same with the $70, which becomes $7,000 we can now do EPS calculations. This means that our Cost of Revenue, which is also our Liabilities in this situation, turns each share into $3000/2000. This makes our EPS 1.5. Now, to get P/E we do:

$$P/E = MarketPrice/EPS$$

Therefore, if we say that the Market Price is $5 and our EPS is 1.5, then our P/E is 3 ⅓. This is important to understand because this means we need 3 ⅓ shares to get us an annual amount of $1.

So, now that we have worked through this, you understand the general gist of most of the stock market. Good investors will look for a low P/E value and a medium to high Margin of Safety. While there's definitely a bit more to stock trading, this book is about Financial Machine Language and how it relates to the stock market.

Why You Need to Know How It is Calculated

Information is Not Real-Time

The most important part of this is that you needed to know the previous information because even if you rely on the information gathered at stock market APIs, they may not have the most recent, updated information. For instance, a common trick to see if the information is updated daily or updated in real-time is to check the P/E value for yourself. Sometimes, the number for this could be one or two points lower or higher than what you personally calculate, which means what you calculated is more accurate than the information you're being provided with.

You Need to Teach the Machine This

You need to actually teach this to the machine, so all the equations you would normally do in a financial situation needs to be done by the machine itself. After all, what is the point of building a machine learning neural network if the neural network cannot function in its original purpose? You can use machine learning to identify Trends and similar, simple tasks. However, if you're going to spend the time to train a neural network, it might be worth your effort to build a machine that could suggest trades rather than look at common market trends and just provide general data you already have access to.

You Need to Know Where to Point the Machine

No matter what you are doing with a machine learning algorithm, you are going to need a way to point it in a certain direction. Whether you plan to use the machine to identify trends, to identify companies worth investing in, to see if there are hidden relations between companies, or anything else, you need to at least know the mathematics used in the stock market so that you can effectively point the machine towards the direction you wanted to go.

Understanding How a Trader will Trade

Now we get to the **point** of *this* chapter, but we first needed to set up a base to understand this. When you develop a machine learning algorithm for financial purposes you need to know what you will be using to teach that machine learning algorithm. If the machine learning algorithm doesn't know how to make the proper Financial choices, it doesn't make sense to make a machine learning algorithm or try and use one to replace your own decisions. Therefore, now that you know how the different stock strategies work and the math that goes along with the stock market in general, we will now go over the different parts you need to build in a machine learning algorithm.

Point-of-Direction

While most might think that the Point of Direction is "most profit", but this is not how a stock trader thinks. In fact, "most profit" is a benefit of what they actually think of. Most stock traders will focus themselves on undervalued assets, currently expensive trends, and what's currently selling for fair value.

There's really a benefit to each of these, depending on how you handle them. For instance, the easiest one to think about is finding undervalued assets but it is the most difficult to resolve. The previously mentioned method in Positional Trading is actually referred to as the Warren Buffett way of trading. You calculate what's currently undervalued if they have a low P/E and BV. This tells you that you will get a lot of money for anything you purchase, but there's more to this story. For instance, what if you were trying to find an undervalued new piece of science?

27

It was generally thought of as a hobby practice in the 1960s. Only Rich individuals could really invest money in this and you had to order it through very selective magazines. In addition to this, those magazines usually funded the project themselves. This was a fairly complex item to put together and normally it wouldn't make anybody any money because the parts were so expensive. Now, would you invest in this hobby? If you said no, you would have been part of the crowd that didn't profit off of the future of computing. This was a fairly simple example of when undervalued technology enters the marketplace and people don't see the potential future. More importantly, how exactly do you put a value on such an item beyond visionary? The truth of the matter is you simply can't.

The easiest to define is actually allowing a machine learning algorithm to spot currently expensive trends. For instance, how would you identify a trend? You would likely look at the previous data and see that there is a threshold for an upper bounce and a threshold for a lower bounce. This can be easily defined inside of a machine learning algorithm because thresholds are usually what it works in the first place.

You see a particular stock begin to rise and then fall and then repeat this pattern for a few steps, which ultimately leads to a great rise and then a great fall. This is usually referred to as a trend where the company gains a little bit of value and loses a little bit of value but every once in a while, it gains a lot of value and then loses a lot of value. This practice is known as Trend trading and it is fairly common for people who want to make a lot of money quickly but not spend their time watching the stocks on a daily basis. Sure, Trend trading can happen on a daily basis but when you're working with certain companies, these trendlines can actually take weeks to develop. It's not really something that you can predict beyond past patterns of how fast that happened in the past and what caused those events.

Finally, you could simply set the machine learning language to identify sections where the amount is of a fair value and that is to say that it is about equal to what it should be. This is actually pretty hard to do because once a company gets pretty popular, this fair value tends to be thrown out the window. A perfect example of this is the Bitcoin as it is worth far more than what most people would generally say it's worth.

29

In fact, it's usually referred to as a new type of Fiat money because of its initial value and then it's true value being so different.

The problem here is that I can't tell you exactly what point of Direction you should use because it's too difficult to determine the best move. There are better moves that you can make. For instance, you definitely want to try and find the cheapest type of asset that you can get and you definitely want to make sure that you trade in for stocks at a decent value. However, that limit and benefit is really defined by you.

Entry Trading Price

The entry trade is really just the name you use to describe the moment you would find a stock acceptable to buy. In such an instance, you might want to buy stocks at around 20% of the value that they are currently being sold at. This would be a threshold that you would set inside of the computer to determine that you want to buy it at a certain price. The problem here is that you run into an infinite possibility issue. Let's say that you set it to only buy stocks if they are 20% lower in value than when the stocks first opened. Sure, let's say that your machine will now do this and that you, in fact, receive a windfall of stocks because the stock value has gone down by that much, but what happens if it goes down another 20% because the stock market value is crashing for that particular business? That's a huge risk to take and yet it is a very real possibility. Even worse, this could have been any percentage that you said ahead of time because even if you said it to 5%, it could very well go down another 5%.

Additionally, you run into the other side of the problem, what happens if it never goes below that amount? You would then need to adjust it to the amount you felt appropriate, which would likely be based on the lowest common price that it drops to. However, you run into the issue happening again. It is rare, but it does happen, and these are the things you need to think about when going with machine learning and determining your prices for your stocks. After all, you don't want to buy a stock that is plummeting into the ground and you also don't want to have a machine that will never buy any stock because it never reaches the threshold you have set. However, the Entry Trading Price represents the *identification* of a buy-worthy item.

Exit Trading Price

You're going to need to define a trading price in which you exit the market, which is to say that you need to find a price that you are comfortable selling at. Once again, you come into the problem of trying to determine a value that most people determine at the time of looking at the stocks. However, we actually do this all the time in stock trading. This is often referred to as stop order and limit order. For instance, in a stop order, you may only want to buy or sell an item at a specific amount. Until that amount is reached, no money leaves your pocket. In a limit order, we are dealing with the same thresholds a machine language will have to deal with.

A limit order is a type of order that allows you to set a minimum or a maximum for which you will buy and sell at. These are usually speculative numbers that you think the price of the item will reach in a given time period. For instance, let's say that you decide to buy Facebook stock at around $70 per stock. You think, according to pass data, that there is a likelihood that your stock will reach a total of $75. However, you will see that it is possible for your stock to become worth

$65. Based off of your trading strategy, if you invested in Trend trading, you might think that a big Surplus will likely lead to a huge debt. You can then set a limit order to buy the stock at specific quantities, which we will talk about in a little bit after the price of the stock has gone below $65. Likewise, if you do see your stock become worth $75, you can set a limit order to sell that stock once it goes past $75. As you can see, you can set the thresholds of the machine language algorithm to utilize limit orders much the same way that the standard stock trader might.

The Exit Trading Price represents the *identification* of an item worth selling. It's fairly important to recognize that when dealing with machine languages, you have to identify the boundaries before you can use them. With the entry trading price, you are finding products that are worth buying. With the exit trading price, you are evaluating items you have already bought and determining whether it is time to sell them or not.

The Tolerance Range

The reason why I pointed out that the entry trading price is identifying items that are worth buying and the exit trading price are identifying items you already have that are worth selling, is to modulate the machine language algorithm. In both instances, you may follow similar steps, but the data set is significantly smaller for the exit trading price and the mathematics are in reverse to that of the entry trading price. The purpose of these two variables are to identify the upper bound threshold and the lower bound threshold, which requires two separate lanes of logic and data sets.

The Quantity of Sale

Finally, even though it seems obvious, I believe I need to ensure that you understand that one of the key components of any machine learning algorithm dealing with stocks is how to determine how much to sell. While the new stock trader might think that it is a good idea to sell all of their stocks once those stocks become profitable enough, that isn't always the case. For instance, let's say that you have 1,000 stocks inside of Intel. If the stocks rose by $5 then you would have a profit of

$5000 if you sell those. However, if you plan on seeing a possible $20 P/S return, you may only want to sell a few of them while they are profitable and wait to see if the price increases further. After all, sometimes there is an increase in the trend that will eventually lead to a greater downfall, but you can still make quite some money if you look for a climbing trend. Therefore, you may just want to sell 500 of your stocks so that you at least get $2,500 as a profit and then wait to see if it falls back down, which you can then use the profit to buy the stocks at a lower price while waiting for the stocks to climb back up. This allows you to make more money while also keeping reserve stock for when the price is even higher. This means you could have more than one neural network handling portions of stock with different limit orders on them.

Machine Learning to Determine Value of Current Stocks

Training Your Machine Learning Algorithm Quarterly not Annually

Now, you might think this is a bit odd, but when you begin to think of long-term investment, you should really be looking at quarterly reports. However, a normal stock trader will not look at quarterly reports unless they absolutely have to. This is because the quarterly reports can usually be summed up in the financial statistics provided by their chosen stocks' website, which are much easier and quicker to look at. Long-term investment means that you need to find a safe pattern with a specific company to see if it is within acceptable ranges of doing business with.

For instance, as I mentioned before, a company with a great PE value is usually a company that's worth looking into. You then look into the company and find that they also have a great PBV value. This means that the company might be worth investigating, but the problem is that the PE value changes over time. While you may be looking at the current PE value, the past PE values also have, ironically, value. You see, the PE value and other variables can be looked upon over the course of time to determine the overall success of that company. Ideally, you want companies that have the same value or similar value overall.

This is because a company that is worth investing in for the long-term has to have a stable monetary environment. Once you look at the PE value, you might also want to look at the equity that the company has held over those quarterly amounts. While the PE value can tell you how much money you will make by investing with such a company, the equity will help determine the viability of the company. Additionally, a company that may have a decent PE value might also not be able to handle their debt very well or invest back into the company so that the company makes even more money. These are all problems dealing with long-term investment and finding the best companies means that the machine learning algorithm needs to also know which companies in the dataset died and which companies in the dataset lived.

The reason why knowing whether the company is still around or not determines a pattern of death. While it may be somewhat not surprising, companies tend to die in very much the same way. Normally, what will happen is that the company will suddenly have a negative value in their revenue. Now, they could also sell all of their assets before the negative value appears or afterward if they weren't expecting it. This key moment represents when a company is panicking because then the natural pattern is to consistently take on more debt as the company just dwindles into death. On a rare occasion, they do survive, but more often than not most of them will die in very much the same way. Understanding that debt and total revenue play a key role in determining when a company is about to die is key to teaching Machine Learning algorithms to stay away from companies that exhibit the same patterns on a quarterly basis. So, your Dataset may look something like this

Date	P/E Ratio	Total Revenue	Debt	Asset Value	Liability Value	-1 = Dead; 1 = Alive

The Common Sense Method: Trend Trading

The most common method of trading is to use peaks and troughs, which is really just to say that one would follow the Trend. Whether you are looking at the Long Term or Short-Term Investing, you are still looking at Trends. In fact, early on I mentioned that there are 4 primary methods of trading, but in reality, all of them still fall underneath Trend Trading.

Let us take a look at the following chart for the Dow Jones in June of 2018 thanks to CNBC:

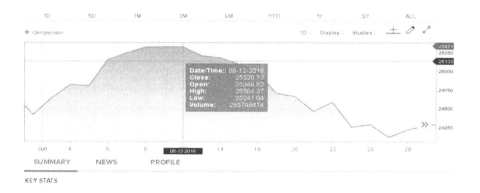

As you can see, this could be one of the better or worse months depending on which side of the hill you sold your stock on. We see two specific type of trends in this chart, I will note them as Green and Red lines in the next chart:

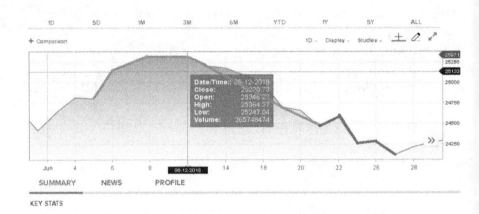

Before, we discussed how to find businesses that were worth investing in during the *Understand How Stocks Work* section. Once you have found a business that's worth investing in, there are 2 different trends all good businesses will experience at different intervals. The Green Line is known as the Big Peak, which is to say that the line will Peak before massively falling. This is the part of the line that people want to sell on. The falling part is known as the Trough Line, which is the area where people wait to buy again. The Red Line is the Little

Peak, where most Day Traders spend their time. It's the same as Big

Peak, but profits come at a much faster pace. If we look at a 6-month

version of this, we can easily see quite a few of these:

This, for us, is fairly easy to understand and becomes a

repeatable pattern we can look for. Provided we are looking at

successful businesses, the models are pretty straightforward and don't

require a lot of math unless you want to become super precise.

The Most Common Machine Learning Method: Support Vector

Regression Algorithm

It is not as simple for Machines to use the same method of

analysis. This is because we have already constructed the algorithms needed to recognize this type of patterns. In fact, the human brain is genetically predisposed to recognize patterns. However, creating a Neural Network is like teaching a toddler how to recognize the same pattern, only machines catch on quicker and require mathematical explanations. Therefore, we have to separate these patterns into two different categories.

The first category is to notice the extremes of the lines, but which ones. Since our brains already recognize the patterns, you might be stuck on thinking of the line, but you need to stop that if you are. The Machine does not see a line, instead, it sees a sequence of positive numbers and we need to retrain the Machine to see something else. It needs to see that positive numbers closer to zero are a **Loss** and positive numbers further away from zero are a **Gain**.

However, you've probably already noticed at there's no good "line" that fits the model. If we look at the previous data, when you define a line for one trend, it will no longer be applicable for another trend. Therefore, we need a way for us to continuously define where the

Losses and Gains are on a Line, which is where Support Vectors come in.

The Support Vector algorithm sets a margin for Gain and a margin for Loss, which are placed along a Trending line. So, let's use the previous definitions for Gain and Loss. Definitions for these lines are a little bit different though. Instead of going from zero, we go from what's known as a Hyperplane. This is a separate line that places itself between the D+ and D- margins, but these margins are defined by the closest or furthest vectors based on your needs. One category is D+ and the other is D-, based upon what you want. These are just classifications and D is just a placeholder, here is the following graph that demonstrates how Support Algorithms would be displayed:

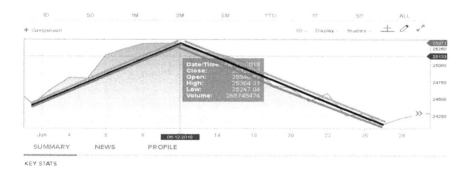

As you can see, the Green Line or D- in our case is the Gain line. The Red Line, on the other hand, represents our Loss line and is the D+ of our equation. Now that you understand the general gist of how it works visually, we'll give a brief explanation of a massively complex algorithm you're going to need to understand what most machine learning stock prediction algorithms will use:

$$y = \sum_{i=1}^{n} (a_i - a_i^*) \cdot \langle \phi(x_i), \phi(x) \rangle + b$$

Don't freak out. It's okay. We're going to walk through this together. You need to understand that this is actually a combination of 2 algorithms. Additionally, this is just an evolved form of

$$y = mx + b$$

Almost all machine learning algorithms start out with the Slope-Intercept and this is because the Slope-Intercept is the first *true* form of Binary Separation. In other words, Slope-Intercept is the same type of formula used in the Perceptron. So, let's go ahead and break this information down into the different components:

$$m = \left(a_i - a_i^*\right)$$

$$x = \langle \phi(x_i), \phi(x) \rangle$$

And I think we can understand that b = b in this situation. So now we're going to break this down even further, but we'll start with x because it is less abstract than m. Let's start with the most confusing part, the angled brackets holding this equation together. You will find these angled breaks when dealing with **Linear Span** and **Linear Algebra**. To understand Linear Span, you must understand **Linear Combination**. A Linear Combination is a combination of Linear Vectors, which is to say if we have a vector of 1 and a vector of 2, this produces a vector of 3 otherwise written as:

$$3 = \langle 1, 2 \rangle$$

Now, the way we would normally write this is

$$\vec{3} = \vec{1} + \vec{2}$$

I would say this makes for an efficient explanation of what's happening with the variables inside of that equation. So, let's rewrite this so it looks a little bit more understandable:

$$x = \phi(\vec{x_i}) + \phi(\vec{x})$$

That little arrow on top represents this as a vector, but now... which vectors and don't vectors come in pairs? Let's address the "pairs" theory because you are technically right but let's think of this in slope form. If you recall, in slope-intercept form, m is a slope, x is x and b is y-intercept. Therefore, a actually refers to slope here, x is not a pair but a single number, and b is still y-intercept. Additionally, one can write (3,1) as x and y, but it can also be written as $(0,0) + (3,0) + (0,1)$ where (0,0) is the origin. Therefore, Vector X is still 3 here, it's just been separated from y and origin is assumed because of the pairs, the zero is the origin and the second is the direction thus (3,0) or 3.

However, in order to understand "which vectors", we have to look at the part of the original equation we have not discussed:

$$\sum_{i=1}^{n}$$

Now, you might be confused by this, but this is really just the mathematical representation of a **for loop** in programming. The $\sum$ part is the Sum of all ns starting at i. Therefore, i represents the current iteration number in the sequence. Just to let you know, this is the **regressive part** as this allows it to iterate through all the vector points in the past by starting at the earliest dated variable. So now we can understand that $\phi\left(\vec{x_i}\right)$ is actually Phi of the current vector for x.

We have explained x so now we need to handle m, which is a little bit more difficult to understand. The part that throws most off is that little asterisk in the corner:

$$\left(a_i^*\right)$$

That asterisk is known as a complex conjugation, which should really be called a reverse or an opposite function because $\left(a_i\right)$ is the opposite. In programming... we would just multiply by -1, am I right? I am **wrong**. It's important to understand how conjugates work. Let's say I have the equation:

$$y = 3x + 2$$

If we multiply everything by -1, I come up with

$$-y = -3(-x) - 2$$

This is **NOT** how conjugation works. In conjugation, I would end up with:

$$\bar{y} = 3x - 2$$

This is an entirely different equation, right? That's because we're locating a number that brings the imaginary number to its' opposite self. If I said x is 1, here's how this would go.

$$\left(y = 3(1) + 2 = 5\right) - \left(\bar{y} = 3(1) - 2 = 1\right) \not\equiv 0$$

Here is the official conjugate formula:

$$x = a + b_i \ \bar{x} = a - b_i$$

In this equation, we have 1 imaginary number and that is b_i where b is the Real number and i is the imaginary number. Therefore, we can only apply the conjugate if the equation looks like:

$$Actual(y = 3x + 2)$$

$$Conjugate(\bar{y} = 3x - 2)$$

So, in the original equation of $\left(a_i - a_i^* \right)$ what we are actually seeing is a Real Number of iteration i minus the Conjugate of the Real Number of iteration i. The last part of this equation is to actually substitute something known as a **Kernel Function**. Now, the most common of these are Polynomial and Gaussian Radial Basis.

Polynomial

$$k(x_i, x_j) = (x_i, x_j)^d$$

Gaussian Radial Basis

$$k(x_i, x_j) = exp\left(-\frac{\|x_i - x_j\|^2}{2\sigma^2} \right)$$

These Kernel Functions allow for Non-linear SVR, which is what we see in the stock market. When using them for this purpose, we use a Kernel Function to replace this

$$\langle \phi(x_i), \phi(x) \rangle$$

If you would like to study SVM more in-depth, here is a great series of web tutorials: https://www.svm-tutorial.com/2014/11/svm-understanding-math-part-1/.

Determine the Optimal Time to Buy Stocks

You Should Not Fully Automate

Now that we have gotten off the beaten path of practically pure mathematical reasoning, I need to tell you upfront that you should not fully automate your trading decisions. There are some that are willing to convince you that fully automated trading is a fantastic idea, but the honest truth is that it's a really bad idea. It's a bad idea because we, as humans, are definitely flawed. What I mean by this is if you didn't train it right, if you missed a line of code, or if something goes wrong in the processing speed, you could make trades you would never make in your entire life.

The problem with developing a machine learning algorithm that's fully automated is that you have to be able to trust that it's going to make the right decision most of the time. The problem with humans is that we are often way too impatient to wait until it can get that good and so we try to use it almost as soon as we build it. The problem with this is you can wind up broke and out of the game within moments of you turning on the machine learning algorithm if you did something wrong. Instead, you should really be using it like a personal advisor at times. Specifically, you should know more than it for a little bit down the road after you have created it.

The moment that you can feel comfortable handing over your trading decisions to the machine should be when it gets the calculation right more than you do. Therefore, say you were to get signals from the machine learning language algorithm that told you that you needed to buy stock and you refuse to do so because it didn't make sense to you, but it turns out that the machine was right. If this happens more than 75% of the day, I would highly recommend just leaving the trading decisions up to the machine because at that point it's more successful than you. However, it's going to take quite some time for it to get up to that type of accuracy and a lot of practice. I would not trust the machine to make any trading decisions within at least the first six months of the machine's creation.

Using Support Vector Regression Analysis to Find Good Times

While Support Vector regression analysis is definitely a fantastic technique, you have to remember that it is it's only designed to predict the next step in the Trends. Therefore, it can actually tell you what times are going to be good for selling and buying your stock. However, it can only ever predict the next step in the process so if it's wrong then it has to recalculate everything until it becomes right. Considering the sheer randomness of the market, it's going to be recalculating quite a bit so while you can use it to find good times to sell your stock, it's not going to be 100% reliable.

We have not gotten to the point where machine learning is more efficient at humans at doing particular tasks 100% of the time. There are certain machine learning applications that can claim that they do it better than humans most of the time, but none of them have significantly proven to be flawless compared to humans. This means that you can utilize it to try and find times to sell the stock in real time, but there are a few other methods out there that can help you determine great times to sell stock.

Specifically, I'm talking about partitioning cluster methods. Partitioning cluster methods are clustering techniques that allow you to separate information into clusters. Therefore, if you are able to find profit spots more than loss spots, you can actually see a pattern of when it's good to sell a certain stock with a company.

For instance, let's say that we divided our information into 30-minute increments for a specific business over the period of a day. During that time, we record moments where the company is at a profit and moments when companies are at a loss. We can actually do this in a line graph, but clustering techniques are specifically meant to grab data points that form into a cluster. Therefore, while you could see a trend line in said 30 minutes, you are more likely to see dots of profit and dots of loss. Therefore, as a natural result, you can actually find the parts of the day where there are more profit dots more often than there are loss dots.

Using Cluster Analysis to Find Good Businesses

Half the battle in determining what companies to sell with and at what times you can sell at is often the business itself. You don't really want a business that is dealing with a massive pile of debt that it can't seemingly pay off. You also don't want a company that if it died yesterday, you would likely only see a small portion of money go back into your pocket. While support vector regression analysis is really good at finding the trend times that you want to sell your stock at, you primarily want to use partitioning and cluster algorithms to determine which companies you should go with.

While we will get into specific clustering methods later on when we discuss penny trading and day trading, clustering algorithms allow you to group together common companies. Therefore, let's say that you have companies that do extremely well, companies that do generally well, companies that do okay, companies that are losing a little bit of money, companies that are losing a lot of money, and companies that are about to die. Now, there are also over a million of these companies and you can't possibly check them all within a reasonable amount of time. Normally, you would generally just look for the best ones that you can cherry-pick out of the data set. This is a problem because you could have missed all of the ones that could make you money, it just gives you the ones that are most popular because, as humans, we are very biased. By using cluster algorithms, we can use the variables that we would normally use to identify companies in those categories and then cluster them on each variable so that we can compare those groups rather than individual companies.

This allows us to group companies together with other companies with the same traits and values without spending a lot of time looking at the data ourselves. To do this, you don't actually need any machine learning algorithm, you need cluster algorithms that take data and make relations to it. This is actually the first step utilized in machine learning to create labels that the machine learning algorithm can then use.

Using this for High Volatility Stocks

This method is actually still pretty useful when considering it for high volatility stocks. High volatility stocks are usually the bane of the existence for the average stock trader, primarily because of how unpredictable they are. The problem is that it has been proven in the past that high volatility stocks can be predictable if you look in the right places. High volatility stocks are almost unanimous with penny stocks and it's because of how penny stocks work. Therefore, primarily you want to look for the same aspects that you would look for in a penny stock business as you would with normal high volatility stocks because you'll find that the similarities are very apparent. That isn't to say that there's not a difference between high volatility stocks and penny stocks, but you look for the same parameters for both because that's usually how you assess whether those stocks are going to make you money or not.

Machine Language Algorithm to Predict Whether to Sell a Stock

Trade Signals are Safe

The safest way for a machine language algorithm to help determine whether you should sell a stock or not is to set it up to give you trade signals. This works in very similar ways to the stop orders and the limit orders that people use to take advantage of automated trading but with the ability to make the decision yourself. For instance, you can get a trade signal that tells you that a current stock price is worth selling at that time. If the machine was allowed to make the trade for you, you would sell your stock at the moment the signal would normally go off. The reason why I think this is crucial to understand this is that you could make more money if you waited longer after the trade signal.

A normal stock trader will have one of three options when dealing with an automated trading system. The first option is that the trader doesn't use the network at all, this is often referred to as the

imaginary choice. The second option is that the trader uses the machine

language algorithm to give the stocks trader advice. The last option is

for the stock trader to fully trust the machine to make trade decisions on

behalf of the stock trader.

Having a Machine Trade For You Pros

There are a few benefits that come with allowing the machine to

make decisions for you. The first benefit that I would say that machines

have over humans is the ability to make that Split-Second sale. There is

a period of time where the user may take longer to make a stocks

decision, and this can actually lead to a loss of money if the decision

isn't made fast enough. Additionally, this lends to the fact that machines

are faster at analyzing information than humans and that's simply

because they are built to only do that whereas humans have a whole

bunch of mechanisms for survival that get in the way.

This actually leads this to the secondary benefit and that is really

that machines don't have emotions. For instance, a person will probably never invest in a company that they hate no matter how profitable that they may be. That isn't to say that the person doesn't want to make money, it's just their emotions are getting in the way of making the money. Machines don't have that problem and all they care about are executing the tasks that are given to it via programming. Therefore, machines are more open to the types of trades that they can make whereas humans purposely limit themselves based on their emotional background and their history.

The last benefit that I would say that machines have over humans is that they can analyze bulk information far quicker than humans. This is different than the split-second sale that I was talking about before. A lot of information goes in beforehand to determine whether a company is worth investing in or not and humans have to look up the numbers and do the research themselves. A machine that has access to an API of information will actually be able to analyze those numbers based on the parameters that the human set beforehand. While it may take a human nearly a week to study and determine the worthiness of companies that match his profile, it may take a machine an hour or two at most. This makes them highly efficient at finding good companies quickly and then putting into action good policies to make their owner's money.

Having a Machine Trade For You Cons

There's one huge disadvantage that comes with having a machine trade for you and a lot of other little disadvantages. The one huge disadvantage is that once it starts to mess up, it cannot stop itself. A machine is designed to continuously run and if it makes a wrong choice and the mathematics are devolving, it continues to devolve into whatever mess is you wind up catching it at. This means that you could be a millionaire and if you let a machine control your money and that machine begins to mess up, you may not catch it until you're broke. This is a huge problem that belies all types of Technology but especially machine learning technology. This is why you have to spend months testing the software before you can trust it. You have to constantly make sure that your choices would line up with the machine's choices and vice versa.

This actually brings me into my second point and that is that it takes a lot of time to make sure that a machine learning algorithm is up to par with what you would do. You need to take time out of your day to invest in the machine learning algorithm so that you can test it, correct it, and perfect it. It takes months and even years to make a machine learning algorithm that won't eat itself when it starts to mess up and will provide you with accurate information. This is why most people leave it up to big corporations that make money off of this software because they allow those corporations to invest their time and the person paying them is saving time by allowing the company to do it for them.

Now, there are a whole bunch of other problems that come with developing a machine learning algorithm. I won't list them here because I could actually write an entirely different book on the problems that can happen with machine learning, but there is a litany of issues that a developer has to deal with when handling machine learning algorithms. Yes, most people will brag about how machine learning is awesome and how machine learning can basically solve every problem on the planet, but the machine learning itself is a very tiresome and difficult science to put into practice. It takes a lot of patience but, usually, the payoff is generally worth the amount of work required to put in.

It's Really All about Predicting the Trend

The last thing that I want to say here is that this is really all about predicting the Trend. Every single thing in this book is really just about predicting where the trend line is going to be and how you can use machine learning to predict that trend line. That Trend line is how we make money, which machines are really good at predicting because we use mathematics to predict it ourselves.

Determine Value of a Penny Stock

Long History Data is Not Good

Ironically, a penny stock is one of the very few stock options that you don't want a lengthy history about. The reason being is that penny stock is usually penny stock because either the company just started or the company is barely on the stock market radar because of reasons. Often, I find that the reason why many companies are on the penny stock list is simply that they were worth a lot of money and then they got into a lot of trouble that eventually plummeted their overall worth. Most times, I've seen companies go from $60 or $100 all the way down to $3 within the span of maybe a year.

This means that if you were to feed in the information to the machine learning algorithm from a long history, the machine would learn of the huge losing gap that occurs with penny stocks. In fact, if you based your profit margins off of past iterations, you might actually see that you may never buy penny stock as a result. Now, most of the penny stock makes you money through bulk purchases. That is to say, if the stock is worth somewhere around $0.27, if you buy a hundred of that stock, you now have around $270 in that stock. If that stock goes up by a single penny, you then go up by $10 as a result. This is where the money is for penny stocks; bulk orders of the stock because any fluctuation towards the positive usually means you're getting massive benefits.

The problem is really determining whether a company is dwindling and dying or if the company might make a comeback. It's kind of sad to say, but the penny stock is really the market where the average stock trader is kind of rooting for the underdog at that point. These are companies that have been at the height of their game and something happened to where they're almost next to worthless on the stock market. The stock traders in this stock market are using and taking advantage of the cheap prices to make multiplicative dollars off of pennies, which actually helps keep those companies alive. Remember, when the stock goes up, it usually means that the actual value of the company goes up as well. Therefore, successful trading in stocks with the company that is in penny stocks might actually bring them back to their height of glory that they once knew.

Beside that sentimental view, you are defining the successes based on pennies and not dollars, so your thresholds need to take this into account. If your stock originally started at $70 5 years ago and is somewhere around $0.50 nowadays, you are not looking to make the $70 that that company once had. You don't want to overload your machine learning algorithm with useless information. This would mean that you are able to train your machine on data sets quicker because it is only data that is the most useful. Likewise, you really shouldn't need more than a year or two to gauge the success of certain penny stocks.

History of Debt is Good

On the flip side of things, just as you don't necessarily want a long history on the company and its profits, you do want a history of debt. You see, one of the key factors inside of penny stocks is whether that the company is dying. The one thing that you look out for is a company that is surviving and a company that is continuing to die. You see, a company that is surviving will eventually rise back up and that's the ultimate wish for a penny stock trader because if you have a hundred stocks that you bought at $0.27 and the company rises to a stock value of $30, you spent $270 to make three grand. That's a huge amount of money but it's usually way too risky to do that. Instead, what you do is you look for the trends of the day.

Just like with most trading, you want to look for Trends in the data itself and you want to make sure that you are only looking at trends for companies that are surviving. This means that you don't necessarily want to look at all the companies you can inside of the penny stock market. Instead, what you want to do is you want to filter out all of the companies that have an unmanageable debt. The way that you do this is you collect information on equity for all of the companies. You then set up a margin that you find acceptable for equity levels. You can also throw in total revenue to see if they are surviving by subtracting the total revenue and the equity, but essentially you want to make sure that you capture the debt and you want to pay attention for debt that is decreasing. Decreasing debt means that the company is starting to come back. You won't necessarily see a revenue spike because the company is struggling and is probably making the same if not a little bit less than what they're used to.

This debt history can actually be used to calculate the company's margins of risk. Therefore, if a company has a massive amount of debt and it doesn't seem to be lowering, the machine can use clustering to put that debt area into a specific graph that's away from the others. You could also have it separate the margin of risk by percentages so that if it fits within a certain percentage then the clustering can bring that into groups so that you can easily identify which ones have high debt that's being managed and which ones have low debt that are doing okay and then you have ones in the middle that aren't able to seem like that they're getting rid of that but the debts not increasing. What this does is that it creates categories of risk that you can easily identify as companies worth investing in. The reason why you might want to use clustering for this is because of the sheer amount of data that you have to go through. You may have to only look at a single number, but you also have to look at a single number 8 times for each company that you're going through and you're likely to go through at least a thousand. That means you're literally looking at around 8,000 numbers, which would be quicker if you simply used a clustering technique to auto sort them.

As A Day Trader

The difference between penny trading and day trading is a little bit different in how you go about it, but also very much the same. You are still looking at variables such as debt and you are looking at debt history, but you are also including the link to your history that you would not normally include with penny trading. This is due to the fact that as a day trader, you are not looking at just companies that are trying to survive but companies that are making a decent profit. Therefore, you are looking for very much the same variables but for a different reason.

This means that you might have to tweak your algorithms slightly so that you include extra variables in your classifications. You primarily want to look at the companies that are making a decent amount of money, have a decent margin of safety, and have a considerable P/E ratio. Once you develop a machine learning algorithm that takes these into account, you can then further develop it so that it takes other variables into account and thus becomes more precise. However, this is how you might create the machine learning algorithm to make very quick assumptions as to companies that are worth your time within minutes of you giving it data. In my honest opinion, I would probably have three different machine learning algorithms running at different times because this allows different variations of knowledge to be coming through. I would have your standard Financial machine learning algorithm running and using all the variables I would normally use to judge a company, a machine learning algorithm that just determines whether the company is surviving or thriving versus dying, and a final algorithm that determines trending companies at that time. These will give you, mostly, different results but the sweet spots are the companies that fit into 2 categories, primarily trending with the first or second ML algorithm.

Clustering Techniques

Partitioning is your Friend

I've already shown you how to choose the best times but we both know that the best way to determine a company is if it shows similar features. Therefore, we look at the PE ratio, debt, total revenue, and many other distinctive features. Now, if you are searching through thousands if not millions of companies, it's going to be difficult to look at each and every variable. Let's say that you were only looking at five variables for the company, you would then need to look at 5 million variables if you went with millions of companies and 5000 variables if you were dealing with thousands of companies. Lastly, you would then also need to take note of which companies were good and which companies were bad. Therefore, you may actually accidentally check the same company twice and waste time doing that.

The best way to figure out which company is worth time investment is really to utilize the same variables that you would look at and run a partitioning algorithm on them. Specifically, on each of the variables you would look at, you would run a partitioning algorithm. Therefore, you would look at a clustering algorithm that organizes all of the PE ratios according to randomize spots so that you have high PE ratios, medium PE ratios, and low PE ratios. You could do this with total revenue, debt, and pretty much any of the other variables. However, they are not going to be your final conclusion. Since you compare all of the numbers together, you then take the companies that are put into the categories that you like the most and do the comparison that way. What it does is it shrinks down the number of companies that there are to a group of companies that you can make assessments of based off of comparisons.

1. Cluster like-variable companies

2. Extract companies with Preferred variables

3. Use standard comparative statistics on those companies to determine the value

K-Means Clustering

K-means clustering is actually a really simple, reiterative technique based on mean calculations. For every category of data you want to measure, you place a randomized "centroid". You then calculate the distance from each datapoint to each centroid and create a relation to the nearest centroid for that datapoint. Once this is done for all centroids, you calculate for the mean of each cluster. Using the mean of each cluster, we recluster using the mean values to measure the distance rather than the randomized value we started out with. Finally, if that doesn't change the clustering, then we calculate and keep track of the variation between the clusters. It will repeat this process as many times as you want, but only return the one with the best variation.

The primary problem with this algorithm is that it's sensitive to outlier data. Therefore, if you have companies that have huge amounts of debt, they are likely to throw off your results. If you really want this to work, you have to run through this algorithm, see what it produces, and if you notice that you are getting skewed results, you need to find the companies with the huge amounts of debt and remove them. So, if you notice that a company with $60k of debt is in the same group as the company with $900k of debt, you know that the second company is an outlier. You can learn more about K-means clustering here: https://www.datascience.com/blog/k-means-clustering .

K-medoids

This algorithm does very much the same thing as the previous clustering algorithm, however, it is less sensitive to outliers because of the medoidshift algorithm. The only problem and the main reason why this algorithm is not very popular is due to the computational requirements that it needs to do. Therefore, if you are iterating over hundreds, thousands, or even millions of companies, it's going to take you significantly longer to make the necessary calculations to get to the end result when compared to the first algorithm that I listed here.

You can find out more about K-medoids here: http://www.math.le.ac.uk/people/ag153/homepage/KmeansKmedoids/K means_Kmedoids.html .

CLARANS

Due to the lack of optimization of the k-medoids algorithm, there have been many redesigns for how the algorithm goes about doing the same calculation. This algorithm stands for Clustering Large Applications with Randomized Search. This means that it is specifically designed to run a very similar version of the previous algorithm, but it's also changed so that it is better for large-scale applications.

Best software to automate your trading decisions

A Quick Notice

Much of the applications that I list here I will say that you can get a lot of information from. You have to realize before you try to go get that information that I am talking about information interception, which is a lot different than just accessing information. Information interception is where you figure out how the information is being aggregated into a program and then you intercept that information for your own uses. It's not necessarily hacking, but a lot of people would view it in the same light. Now, there are some software here that does not require that you do information interception but most of the software are all-in-one platforms where the user is not expected to need anything else outside of the platform. Therefore, the digital infrastructure is not necessarily there for some of us who want the information these programs are delivering.

Fully Automated Online Trading: Wealth Simple

Wealthsimple is by far the best in its' category because it

literally handles everything, but it does come at a cost of 0.05%

annually as of right now. The reason why it is the best is that it

determines how it will trade based on your current life choices.

Therefore, the older you are the less risk is associated with the profile.

If you are single, it places you at higher risk but if you have a lot of debt

it puts you at lower risk. There's a medium-sized list of pre-applied

options that will determine your risks. Therefore, it is choosing how

your account will trade based on your current lifestyle. The only way it

can determine which options are of the lowest risk is either by using

Machine Learning algorithms or quarterly predictions reports.

You can then determine what you want your profile to trade

into. For instance, if you are an Islamic individual, there are specific

ways in which it is tradition to trade as an Islamist. It has an option to

trade like this that also cooperates with your current risk level. If you

want to invest in the "green" solutions like Tesla and the like, there's

also a plan for that. If you just want it to make more money regardless, there's also that option. It not only determines how risky your trades will be, but you can also let it handle the social responsibility of your profile.

You can put as much as you want into the platform, which means you can start out with $1. It's able to do this by investing in partial shares, which means there's no limit in how much you can invest. However, when you do invest more, you earn more over time. Once you reach over a certain limit, you can then utilize your invested membership to take advantage of certain benefits.

Thinkorswim Ameritrade Practice Software

Starting off with Real Money is a bad idea in most cases if you are new to trading. Additionally, if your machine learning algorithm is new to this game as well, you don't want it handling real money until you know it's good enough to not lose you a ton of money. On top of all of that, it doesn't make financial sense to create your own financial trading software to simulate a stock market just to then make a machine learning algorithm to game it. You run into issues such as trying to make it for the ML algorithm, which means it'll be easier or too hard for it. Generally, you want a software that's meant to train humans how to trade stocks.

This is where Thinkorswim comes into play as it is a significantly complex system that simulates stock trading. In addition to this, it also includes a Paper Money mode, which allows you to trade with Fake Money. This makes it the perfect software to base the construction of the machine learning algorithm off of, provide datasets to the algorithm, and ultimately optimize the algorithm for performance.

It is important for the construction of the machine learning algorithm because of the real-life comparison the software can have. In addition to this, the software is completely biased towards helping stock traders make more money. This means that instead of simply handling a stock market chart, the software provides ups and downs, opens and closes, and many more variables to work with. It's all in one spot, which means that you can siphon the information into the algorithm.

Lastly, the software does not take into account that a machine learning algorithm might be used in conjunction with the software. This means it is neutral for your neural network, which is a best-case scenario.

TradeStation Automated Software

This piece of software is a bit on the pricey side, so you might want to make sure that you have some Deep Pockets before you try to use this software. They do have a simulated service, which means that it is excellent for those who might want to use it to train their models. However, if you go with the service you will need to meet a monthly minimum activity to ensure that your account doesn't become "dead" as they really only want active traders on their platform. This software has a lot of bells and whistles that will make your trading a lot easier if you decide to utilize it instead of having a machine learning algorithm do all of what you need by itself. They have excellent fees whenever you're trying to trade, some of the lowest in the industry and even better for machine learning purposes, they also come with free real-time data on trading if you're into options trading. They've been an outstanding company for years and they have a lot of history, going back all the way to 1982 where they are listed as the first online trading platform. They're not the best but they are really good at providing you with the services you need to get some automated features going. Additionally, they have an extensive macro library and come with a mobile option.

Etna Automatic Trading Software

This is another software that does a really good job at providing a simulator and a mobile option for traders. I included this software on the list primarily because of its customizability and developer friendliness. Unlike many of the options here, you will actually find that this software company advertises more to developers than traders. They have several APIs and web trading capabilities rather than solely being based on desktop technology. This means that if you plan to make your automated trading as a platform, you can actually develop and deploy using their technology without having to create your own brokerage software.

eSignal Automated Trading Software

This software is something that I would call data puke. I don't really use the term very often, but I find that it exquisitely describes how much information comes from this program. You get access to real-time data, like much of the software here, but on top of that, you actually get access to real-time news concerning trade information and a litany of course videos and graphing abilities that I find lacking in many of the other software. While data puke does grant that you will be getting a lot of information, the actual application can be a little bit intimidating once you open it up. This is because almost all of the information is presented to you outright, but just like Gimp, if you spend some time with it, it can actually be a very good software. Likewise, because it is a data puke software, you will have plenty to feed your machine language algorithm if you decide to create one.

Tensorflow

Honestly, if you're really wanting to, you can build your own, but this is going to take quite a bit of time. The software that I've mentioned here are special privilege software and there's a reason why they almost always take a certain percentage of the money. You see, the market is a game of a fee on top of a fee on top of a fee and the pattern continues until it eventually hits you. This means that you are essentially paying the highest fee possible when you go with services like this because they are able to give you the access... at a fee knowing you likely can't go to the market floor. A lot of money is made by providing these platforms and really all they are doing is just providing you with access and information. The more information they can provide you, the more likely you are going to be willing to pay for their platform. This means they have an incentive to pump their software as full of data as possible, which means that a Legion of Developers is really what you're trying to weigh against you developing it on your own. They have experience with the actual software, they have been doing it for numerous years usually, and they know exactly how to incentivize people. Sure, you can develop your own, but it's like trying to make an AAA game by yourself with next to no money to hire anyone else. You can do it, it's just gonna take a really long time.

However, if you plan to make a machine learning algorithm that utilizes their software, then I would highly suggest going with Tensorflow. You see, there are tons of tutorials that will tell you how to make a machine learning algorithm that fits your purposes. Specifically, tutorials on YouTube because tutorials written on a website are usually bookmarked and forgotten. So, you can utilize most of the software here to collect the information that you need and then you can develop a machine learning algorithm that sends input to the application you are aggregating information from. Tensorflow is the easiest way to go about this because they are giving you access to their neural networks and all you have to do is implement the programming logic to take advantage of it. Once you feed the information into the machine, you can actually create an interface that encapsulates the software that you're taking information from and then send the inputs that software is expecting as a click for a buy and a trade. It's up to you really, but it's going to take longer if you try to make the platform yourself and then try to make the machine learning algorithm.

Conclusion

Machine Learning Can Be a Revolutionary Change in Your Life

Machine learning has helped many industries do many things so it's no surprise that in an industry full of numbers, machine learning seems to be on the rise. Machine learning does have a lot of capabilities ahead of it and it has proven to be somewhat successful for many individuals. However, something odd comes up when many people think of the stock market as an unpredictable beast yet we are designing machines to study and sell or buy based off of what they study. This means that the stock market can actually be predictable but within what margin?

Machine learning algorithms are very efficient at what they do. The mathematics needed to understand them literally comes from almost all walks of arithmetic and other libraries of mathematics. The formula that I introduced before had a little bit of linear algebra, a little

86

bit of calculus, and a little bit of geometry in it. It was a huge and scary equation for some yet enlightening for many others.

I would have to say that if you can get machine learning algorithm to work for you, it will be revolutionary to how you handle stocks. In fact, if machine-learning proves to be extremely successful, I think that the average person will begin to engage themselves more with the stock market. A huge barrier with the stock market is simply understanding how it works and it is not easy to find resources that are willing to divulge this information to you. I find this to be ironic because the more people that are in the stock market, the more money that can be made. If the stock market only had one person in it, it wouldn't make any money. However, because millions of people around the world are playing the stock market game, billions to trillions are traded annually.

In addition to this, Stock Market trading may actually just become as commonplace as a checking or savings account. This would be where a person simply puts a certain amount of money in their stocking account and lets the machine make the money. This means that everyone who actively works as a stock trader will essentially no longer need to spend hours and weeks of their time studying the market because we have machines to do that. They will still make money, it's just that many won't find why spending so much time handling the math themselves would benefit them.

Final Thoughts

As I already said, machine learning has many benefits to it and it could be a great opportunity. However, machine-learning is still very much an experimental type of programming. You shouldn't 100% rely on machine learning to make all of your decisions for you because there are huge risks to allowing that to happen. It will take time to train a machine learning algorithm to trade like you trade, but if you give it enough effort, you may find that machine trading is a lot more efficient than trying to trade on your own.

CPSIA information can be obtained
at www.ICGtesting.com
Printed in the USA
LVHW011643070720
659997LV00011B/1133